MW01504476

Man Up! Prayer Journal

Scripture quotations taken from the New American Standard Bible, Copyright © 1960, 1962, 1963, 1968, 1971, 1972, 1973, 1975, 1977, 1995 by The Lockman Foundation Used by permission." (www.Lockman.org)

ISBN 978-0-9839288-2-9

MAN UP AND PRAY

"Pray without ceasing" (1 Thessalonians 5:17).

If you can learn anything from Jesus, it's how to pray. We seem to take this for granted. Which means we are real spiritual sissies when it comes to prayer. Oh, we are very good at the popcorn prayers: "Dear lord, help me with . . . " or "Lord, can You . . . " But we don't take time to really get in touch with God through prayer.

To have a heartfelt conversation with God is something lukewarm Christians have a hard time of doing. Pride, sin, or laziness keeps us from truly communicating with God, and yet this is where we need the discipline the most.

The twelve apostles saw Jesus do miracles, preach great sermons, and stump some of the greatest minds of His time.
But the one thing they asked Jesus was about prayer: "Lord, teach us how to pray."

This prayer journal is meant to help you become disciplined in your prayer life. Start today and write your prayer down just like you want God to hear it. Journal your thoughts, your request and your repentance.

Journaling your prayer life will give you the opportunity to look back and see where God answered your prayers. It will also let you see the prayers where God said no or sometimes He said wait. Whatever the answer was, you will be able to see it, because it's written down.

God bless, Man Up and Pray,

Jody Burkeen, Founder of Man Up Gods Way

Place the date and the scripture you read during your daily
devotion in the spaces above.

Matthew 6:6 *"But you, when you pray, go into your inner room,*
close your door and pray to your Father who is in secret, and your
Father who sees what is done in secret will reward you.

Matthew 6:9 *"Pray, then, in this way: 'Our Father who is in heaven, Hallowed be Your name.*

Matthew 14:23 *After He had sent the crowds away, He went up on the mountain by Himself to pray; and when it was evening, He was there alone.*

_____

_____

_____

_____

_____

_____

_____

_____

_____

_____

_____

_____

_____

_____

_____

_____

_____

_____

_____

_____

Matthew 26:36 *Then Jesus came with them to a place called Gethsemane, and said to His disciples, "Sit here while I go over there and pray."*

Mark 11:24 *"Therefore I say to you, all things for which you pray and ask, believe that you have received them, and they will be granted you.*

Mark 14:35 *And He went a little beyond them, and fell to the ground and began to pray that if it were possible, the hour might pass Him by.*

Luke 5:16 *But Jesus Himself would often slip away to the wilderness and pray.*

Luke 6:12 *It was at this time that He went off to the mountain to pray, and He spent the whole night in prayer to God.*

Luke 6:28 *bless those who curse you, pray for those who mistreat you.*

Luke 18:1 *Now He was telling them a parable to show that at all times they ought to pray and not to lose heart,*

Luke 22:40 *When He arrived at the place, He said to them, "Pray that you may not enter into temptation."*

Acts 8:22 *"Therefore repent of this wickedness of yours, and pray the Lord that, if possible, the intention of your heart may be forgiven you.*

Romans 8:26 *In the same way the Spirit also helps our weakness; for we do not know how to pray as we should, but the Spirit Himself intercedes for us with groaning's too deep for words;*

Ephesians 1:18 *I pray that the eyes of your heart may be enlightened, so that you will know what is the hope of His calling, what are the riches of the glory of His inheritance in the saints,*

Ephesians 6:18 *With all prayer and petition pray at all times in the Spirit, and with this in view, be on the alert with all perseverance and petition for all the saints,*

1 Thessalonians 5:17 *pray without ceasing;*

1 Timothy 2:8 *Therefore I want the men in every place to pray, lifting up holy hands, without wrath and dissension.*

Philemon 1:6 *and I pray that the fellowship of your faith may become effective through the knowledge of every good thing which is in you for Christ's sake.*

James 5:13 *Is anyone among you suffering? Then he must pray. Is anyone cheerful? He is to sing praises.*

James 5:16 *Therefore, confess your sins to one another, and pray for one another so that you may be healed. The effective prayer of a righteous man can accomplish much.*

Psalms 34:11 *Come, you children, listen to me; I will teach you the fear of the Lord.*

Proverbs 5:7 *Now then, my sons, listen to me And do not depart from the words of my mouth.*

Proverbs 8:6 *"Listen, for I will speak noble things; And the opening of my lips will reveal right things.*

Proverbs 8:32 "*Now therefore, O sons, listen to me, For blessed are they who keep my ways.*

Proverbs 19:20 *Listen to counsel and accept discipline, that you may be wise the rest of your days.*

Proverbs 23:22 *Listen to your father who begot you, And do not despise your mother when she is old.*

_____

_____

_____

_____

_____

_____

_____

_____

_____

_____

_____

_____

_____

_____

_____

_____

_____

Ecclesiastes 7:5 *It is better to listen to the rebuke of a wise man than for one to listen to the song of fools.*

Luke 9:35 *Then a voice came out of the cloud, saying, "This is My Son, My Chosen One; listen to Him!"*

Psalms 62:1 *My soul waits in silence for God only; From Him is my salvation.*

Genesis 49:18 *For Your salvation I wait, O Lord.*

Psalms 25:4 *Make me know Your ways, O Lord; Teach me Your paths.*

Psalms 27:14 *Wait for the Lord; Be strong and let your heart take courage; Yes, wait for the Lord.*

Psalms 31:24 *Be strong and let your heart take courage, All you who hope in the Lord.*

Micah 7:7 *But as for me, I will watch expectantly for the Lord; I will wait for the God of my salvation. My God will hear me.*

Hosea 12:6 *Therefore, return to your God, Observe kindness and justice, And wait for your God continually.*

Galatians 2:20 *I have been crucified with Christ; and it is no longer I who live, but Christ lives in me; and the life which I now live in the flesh I live by faith in the Son of God, who loved me and gave Himself up for me.*

Isaiah 40:8 *The grass withers, the flower fades, But the word of our God stands forever.*

Matthew 5:16 *Let your light shine before men in such a way that they may see your good works, and glorify your Father who is in heaven.*

John 16:23 *In that day you will not question Me about anything. Truly, truly, I say to you, if you ask the Father for anything in My name, He will give it to you.*

1 Peter 5:5 *You younger men, likewise, be subject to your elders; and all of you, clothe yourselves with humility toward one another, for God is opposed to the proud, but gives grace to the humble.*

Ephesians 4:15 *but speaking the truth in love, we are to grow up in all aspects into Him who is the head, even Christ,*

2 Corinthians 13:5 *Test yourselves to see if you are in the faith; examine yourselves! Or do you not recognize this about yourselves, that Jesus Christ is in you—unless indeed you fail the test?*

Psalms 91:9 *For you have made the Lord, my refuge, Even the Most High, your dwelling place.*

_____

_____

_____

_____

_____

_____

_____

_____

_____

_____

_____

_____

_____

_____

_____

_____

_____

Mark 10:27 *Looking at them, Jesus said, "With people it is impossible, but not with God; for all things are possible with God."*

Ephesians 5:8 *for you were formerly darkness, but now you are Light in the Lord; walk as children of Light*

Joshua 23:11 *So take diligent heed to yourselves to love the Lord your God.*

Philippians 4:19 *And my God will supply all your needs according to His riches in glory in Christ Jesus.*

James 1:2 *Consider it all joy, my brethren, when you encounter various trials,*

Psalms 145:2 *Every day I will bless You, And I will praise Your name forever and ever.*

Romans 8:28 *And we know that God causes all things to work together for good to those who love God, to those who are called according to His purpose.*

Psalms 25:4 *Make me know Your ways, O Lord; Teach me Your paths.*

_____

_____

_____

_____

_____

_____

_____

_____

_____

_____

_____

_____

_____

_____

_____

_____

_____

_____

Hebrews 4:9 *So there remains a Sabbath rest for the people of God.*

_____

_____

_____

_____

_____

_____

_____

_____

_____

_____

_____

_____

_____

_____

_____

_____

_____

_____

Ephesians 5:23 *For the husband is the head of the wife, as Christ also is the head of the church, He Himself being the Savior of the body*

Ephesians 5:25 *Husbands, love your wives, just as Christ also loved the church and gave Himself up for her,*

Ephesians 5:28 *So husbands ought also to love their own wives as their own bodies. He who loves his own wife loves himself;*

Revelation 3:19 *Those whom I love, I reprove and discipline; therefore be zealous and repent.*

Ephesians 1:13 *In Him, you also, after listening to the message of truth, the gospel of your salvation—having also believed, you were sealed in Him with the Holy Spirit of promise,*

Proverbs 27:2 *Let another praise you, and not your own mouth; A stranger, and not your own lips.*

John 14:6 *Jesus said to him, "I am the way, and the truth, and the life; no one comes to the Father but through Me.*

_____
_____
_____
_____
_____
_____
_____
_____
_____
_____
_____
_____
_____
_____
_____
_____
_____
_____
_____

Philippians 3:13 *Brethren, I do not regard myself as having laid hold of it yet; but one thing I do: forgetting what lies behind and reaching forward to what lies ahead,*

_____

_____

_____

_____

_____

_____

_____

_____

_____

_____

_____

_____

_____

_____

_____

_____

_____

Galatians 6:7 *Do not be deceived, God is not mocked; for whatever a man sows, this he will also reap.*

1 John 1:9 *If we confess our sins, He is faithful and righteous to forgive us our sins and to cleanse us from all unrighteousness.*

Philippians 1:21 *For to me, to live is Christ and to die is gain.*

_____

_____

_____

_____

_____

_____

_____

_____

_____

_____

_____

_____

_____

_____

_____

_____

_____

_____

_____

John 15:5 *I am the vine, you are the branches; he who abides in Me and I in him, he bears much fruit, for apart from Me you can do nothing.*

Romans 8:28 *And we know that God causes all things to work together for good to those who love God, to those who are called according to His purpose.*

Psalms 23:3 *He restores my soul; He guides me in the paths of righteousness For His name's sake.*

_____

_____

_____

_____

_____

_____

_____

_____

_____

_____

_____

_____

_____

_____

_____

_____

_____

_____

_____

_____

_____

_____

Ephesians 5:15 *Therefore be careful how you walk, not as unwise men but as wise,*

Galatians 6:2 *Bear one another's burdens, and thereby fulfill the law of Christ.*

Proverbs 4:18 *But the path of the righteous is like the light of dawn, That shines brighter and brighter until the full day.*

_____
_____
_____
_____
_____
_____
_____
_____
_____
_____
_____
_____
_____
_____
_____
_____
_____
_____
_____

Psalms 62:5 *My soul, wait in silence for God only, For my hope is from Him.*